Tea Bag Folding

Tiny van der Plas and Janet Wilson

Tea Bag Folding

SEARCH PRESS

First published in Great Britain 2001 by
Search Press Limited
Wellwood
North Farm Road
Tunbridge Wells
Kent TN2 3DR

Originally published in The Netherlands 2001 by
La Rivière, creatieve uitgevers, Baarn
Original Title: *Kleurrijk Kaleidoscoopvouwen*

Editor: Anja Timmerman
Photographer: Hennie Raaymakers, Sint-Michielsgestel
Cover design: Studio Jan de Boer, Amsterdam
Lay-out: Paul Boyer, Amsterdam

English translation by Janet Wilson
English translation © Search Press Limited 2001

ISBN 0 85532 969 6

Suppliers
If you have any difficulty in obtaining any of the materials and equipment
mentioned in this book, then please write to the publishers for a current list
of stockists, which includes firms who operate a mail-order service:
Search Press Limited, Wellwood,
North Farm Road, Tunbridge Wells,
Kent TN2 3DR, England

The authors would like to thank the following organisations for supplying
some of the tools and materials used for the projects in this book:
O'Harris, Almere, The Netherlands
Vaessen Creative, Nuth, The Netherlands
Kars & Co., Ochten, The Netherlands
Ranger Industries, Inc. USA
Kaiser-Wilson Enterprises USA/UK

CONTENTS

FOREWORD

We have been good friends and colleagues for ten years and enjoy working together. We had great fun making our first video on tea bag folding and we have thoroughly enjoyed making this, our first book, together. Using the folding papers, cutting papers and matching rubber stamps designed by Janet, we have spent many happy hours together designing and making innovative cards, boxes, books and more. Our joint creativity sparked off lots of different ideas, and we hope that all of you, whether you be stampers, tea bag enthusiasts or general paper crafters, have as many happy, creative hours as we did.

We would like to thank Alice Boëtius, Dorothy Hughes, Lynne Kaiser, Henriëtta van Lunen and Lies Vleeschhouwer for all the help, encouragement and support they gave us during the making of this book.

Our very special thanks are extended to the good sisters of a Brazilian convent, who allowed and encouraged us to alter one of their very old parchment lace patterns for you to enjoy.

Janet Wilson and Tiny van der Plas-van Nunen

NOTE

The authors refer to metric measurements throughout this book. Due to the precise nature of Tea Bag folding it is recommended that the reader should use these.

To convert a measurement given in centimetres (cm) to inches (in) multiply by 0.3937. To convert a measurement given in millimetres (mm) to inches multiply by 0.0394. Some useful conversions are listed opposite.

Metric to imperial		Imperial to metric	
1mm	0.04in	1/16in	1.6mm
2mm	0.08in	1/8in	3.2mm
3mm	0.12in	1/4in	6.4mm
4mm	0.16in	1/2in	1.27cm
5mm	0.20in	1in	2.54cm
1cm	0.39in	2in	5.08cm
2cm	0.79in	3in	7.62cm
5cm	1.97in	4in	10.16cm
10cm	3.94in	5in	12.70cm
15cm	5.91in	6in	15.24cm
20cm	7.87in	8in	20.32cm
25cm	9.84in	10in	25.40cm
30cm	11.81in	12in	30.48cm
35cm	13.78in	14in	35.56cm

GENERAL INSTRUCTIONS

MATERIALS

The following is a list of all the materials used for the projects in this book:

Special papers Folding papers, cutting papers and concentric-circle papers.

Stock papers Origami paper, pastel paper, decorative paper, gift wrap paper, metallic foil, corrugated paper and scrap paper (to practise on).

Stock cards Coloured card, glossy white card, 2mm thick card (or mountboard) and 3mm foam board.

Other materials Clear acetate sheet, metal sheet, wire mesh, ribbon, tracing paper and silver wire.

ADHESIVES

PVA (and cocktail sticks), spray adhesive, petroleum-based rubber solution adhesive, double-sided sticky tape/sheet, all-purpose glue, silicone glue (or self-adhesive tabs) and low-tack tape.

EQUIPMENT

Cutting Craft knife, steel straight edge or cutting rule, cutting mat, paper-cutting scissors, general-purpose scissors, fancy-edged scissors, corner scissors and fancy paper punches.

Rubber stamping Rubber stamps (to match the folding and cutting papers), dye ink pads, embossing ink pad, clear embossing powder (and a heat tool), embossing ink dauber/embossing pen, acrylic paint, a sponge and paper towel.

Paper pricking Pricking tool (No. 5 Sharp sewing needle in a needle vice), high-density foam perforating mat, and a perforating grid.

Embossing 'Fun foam' embossing mat, embossing tools, plastic quilting wheel, metal embossing stencils and paper stumps.

Other Pliers (small, flat- and round-nosed types), tweezers, pencils, ruler, masking tape and a lino roller (brayer.)

FOLDING PAPERS

The projects in this book use sheets of folding papers, each of which has eight 5cm squares and twenty 4cm squares printed on it, but you can also use gift wraps that have small repeat patterns. To make good folds you must cut the paper exactly square and, to help you, the folding papers are printed with guide lines. You can also create entirely different designs by cutting squares from other parts of the sheet (see page 9). The project instructions mention special cuts where necessary. Do not discard any left-overs; you can use these as borders or apertures, or for folds that only require half a folding paper.

International origami symbols have been used on all the folding patterns, and these are explained on page 8. Always look at where an arrow starts and where it goes, then fold the paper in that direction. The patterns are colour coded – a white square indicates that the back or white side of the paper is uppermost, a grey square indicates that the coloured side of the paper is uppermost. Practise the folds on large squares of scrap paper before starting a project.

CUTTING PAPERS

These sheets complement the folding sheets, and have various eight-pointed star or octagonal designs printed on them. You can use these as a base for folding papers, you can layer them to create a fuller faux fold, or you can cut them into segments and use these to decorate projects.

To create a faux fold, make mountain folds across opposite points of the cutting paper shapes, then use scissors to make a series of cuts, from the edge of the valley between each point to just short of the centre of the shape (most cutting papers have guide lines to help you). Layer these shapes together, using a spot of glue in the centre of each piece.

If you want a layered effect, and you do not want to use up your printed images, you can cut out more shapes from origami paper, gift wrap, patterned papers or metallic foil. The easiest way to create exactly the right shape is to use the matching rubber stamps that complement the folding papers.

GLUING

We suggest that you use a cocktail stick to apply tiny dots of PVA to the folded layers before gluing them to the project. If you make a mistake, you can usually open the papers again and correct them. A petroleum-based rubber solution is a good alternative to PVA.

Double-sided sticky tape (available on a roll or as large sheets) or spray adhesives are best for sticking large pieces of paper or card. However, a fold made with sticky tape is well and truly stuck! With spray adhesive, if you are quick, you can often remove the piece and reposition it. Use a lino roller (or brayer) to smooth down glued layers to ensure that all the edges are stuck down firmly.

Use small pieces of double-sided sticky tape or small spots of PVA to build up the layers of of cutting paper shapes to make faux folds.

STAMPING

For many of the projects we have used matching rubber stamps and dye ink to decorate plain papers with shapes and colours that complement those on the folding and cutting papers. We have used embossing inks and clear embossing powder for stamping designs on to glossy paper. For a few projects, only part of a stamp design has been used; to ink up part of a stamp, we recommend using an embossing ink dauber or an embossing pen.

SPONGING

Background colour can be added to a stamped and embossed glossy card by sponging with dye ink. When you have finished sponging, simply rub a clean paper towel over the area and the stamped design will 'pop up' out of the background.

International Origami Symbols

A white diagram indicates that the back of the folding paper is uppermost. A grey diagram indicates that the printed side is uppermost.

Valley folds are denoted by a dashed line. The arrow shows the direction of the fold.

Mountain folds are denoted by a dash-and-dot line. The arrow shows the direction of the fold.

This double-ended arrow indicates that you must make a fold, then open it up again.

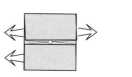

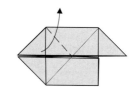

These arrows indicates that you must pull out the underneath layer.

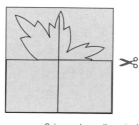

Scissors by a diagram indicates that you must cut the fold to the given shape.

▸ Push in the corner.

↻ Rotate the paper.

⟲ Turn the paper over.

 Repeat previous instruction(s).

RIBBON WEAVING

Some projects include ribbon weaving, visible through an aperture, as part of the design. The weave is assembled on a frame which is then glued to the front or inside of the card. Cut the apertures in the frame and the card at the same time. If the frame is to be mounted on the inside of the card, cut its outer edges approximately 0.5cm smaller than the front of the card to give a neat finish.

Make sure that you weave the ribbon on the correct side of the frame (the side that will be glued to the card). Place double-sided sticky tape around the edge of the frame and remove the protective paper from the top and the left-hand side. Start by sticking one end of the middle vertical ribbon on to the sticky tape, then position the other vertical ribbons on either side. Stick the horizontal ribbons in a similar manner, then weave the ribbons together. Remove the protective paper from the other two sides of the frame, stick the ends of the woven ribbons in position, then trim the ends of all the ribbons so that they do not extend beyond the frame. Place more strips of double-sided sticky tape over the ribbons, then fix the frame to the card.

Use PVA to secure small images to the woven ribbon; apply a tiny spot of PVA on each image, then use tweezers to slip it between the layers of ribbon.

Alternative Cuts for Folding Papers

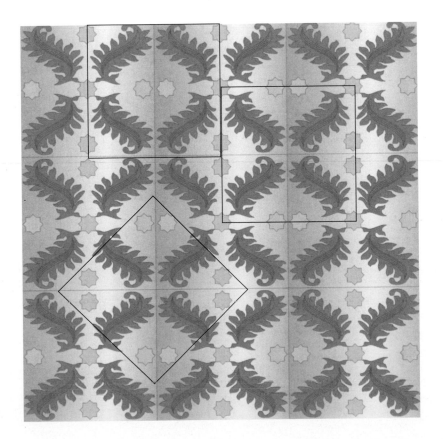

WIRE WORK

Fine silver wire is used to embellish some projects, and to make hangers for others.

Use a small pair of flat-nosed pliers to shape the wire; grip the wire with the pliers where you want the shape to start, make a slight bend, then move the pliers along the wire, extending the shape until you are satisfied with it.

Use small, round-nosed pliers to make eyelets on the ends of the wire. Grip the end of the wire, then turn the pliers to create a circle of wire. Close the circle of wire by carefully squeezing the outer edges. Finally, place the tips of the pliers over the circle and twist it so that it is square to the rest of the wire.

To make a hanger, place the middle of an 8cm length of wire on a pencil or a pen, then wind each end round to create a circle approximately 1cm in diameter. Use flat-nosed pliers to twist the ends of wire together to make a 1cm stem. Open out the tails of the wire and glue these to the project.

WORKING WITH METAL SHEET

The metal sheet we used for the projects in this book has a coating which stops it oxidising, making it perfect for general craft purposes. It is thin enough to emboss shapes or patterns into it, and it can be cut with a heavy duty craft knife or scissors.

To emboss the metal use 'fun foam' as an embossing pad and a paper embossing stylus. In some projects, where we want to emboss elements that complement the designs on the folding and cutting papers, we use the matching rubber stamps and dye ink to print the shapes on the back of the metal. To emboss the metal, place it face down on the foam pad and run an embossing stylus around the printed image. Sometimes, only part of a design needs to be embossed, so refer to the pattern and/or the photograph for guidance. Dye ink can be wiped off the metal with a piece of paper towel. When multiple embossed images are required, stamp and emboss the main image first then work on the next.

When you need to fully raise an embossed design such as that for the Checkerboard Card on page 28, use a metal embossing stencil. Secure the stencil to the right side of the metal with low-tack tape. Place the metal on the foam pad, with the stencil upper-most, then trace round the required shape with a small embossing tool. Turn the metal and stencil face down on the pad (you can now see the outline of the shape you need to raise), then, working slowly and smoothly, use a paper stump or a large-ball plastic embossing tool to raise the image.

You can use a paper embossing tool and a stippling technique to create a textured design on metal such as that for the Star Suncatcher on page 60. Cut out the shape from the metal, place it face down on the foam pad, then tap the tip of the embossing tool randomly over the surface to give a 'hammered' effect on the right side of the metal.

The star-like embossed shapes on the project piece are made using different sizes of miniature drill bits, fitted into a retracting pencil instead of the pencil lead. Keep the tool upright and rotate it so that all the teeth on the drill make contact with the metal. Do not press too hard or you will punch straight through the metal. Practise on a spare piece of metal first.

Use a plastic quilting wheel (as used by sugar paste crafters) and a ruler to make the straight lines of raised dots on the metal layer of the cover for the Triangular Book project on page 33.

FANCY SCISSORS AND PAPER PUNCHES

Fancy-edged scissors and paper punches can give that finishing touch to a project. We have used a few of the many designs that are available. When using the scissors or punches to create straight-line decoration, draw a pencil line on the back of the card and use this as a guide (it can be erased afterwards).

With paper punches, work upside down so that you can see exactly where you are placing the punched shape. Photocopy the pattern from the book and secure it to the paper with low-tack tape or rubber solution adhesive. Remove the debris catcher from the punch then, holding the punch so that the shaped aperture is uppermost, centre the punch over the image on the pattern and punch it out.

MAKING BOXES

Some projects involve making boxes. If the box is made from custom-stamped glossy card, decorate enough card to complete the project. Any left-over pieces can be used to decorate other cards. Cut out the shapes from the patterns provided and carefully fold them along the marked fold lines. Good folding ensures a perfectly shaped box. Rectangular and square boxes have tabs that make up the corners. Use double-sided sticky tape or an all-purpose adhesive for the best results.

The lid and base of the Star Box project on page 25, are made from 3mm thick foam board as this gives a better edge to glue the sides to. Smear all-purpose glue around the edge of the base and top, then, making sure that you line up the star points with the points of the folds, carefully attach the sides. Use all-purpose glue to make the joins in the card. Finish off the lid and base by spray gluing star shapes (cut from the custom-stamped glossy card) on to the foam board.

The box on page 43 has corrugated sides glued to the original smooth sides. To ensure that the lid fits properly, the corrugated sides the base should only extend up to the bottom of the lid. Place the lid on the box, draw a pencil line round the bottom edge of the lid and size the corrugated sides to this line. When you have made up the box, colour the sides by sponging with acrylic paint or dye ink.

MAKING BOOKS

When covering books with paper, you must include flaps at the top, bottom and sides that are folded over and glued to the inside of the covers. You can hide these flaps (and make the inside covers neater) by gluing on 'end papers'. You can make these from plain or stamped paper, from matching folding paper or from gift wrap.

For the CD Holder on page 30, we used custom-stamped paper for the front and back covers, allowing for 1cm flaps. We spray glued the end papers, cut from matching folding paper (0.5cm smaller than the cover) to give a neat finish. Use the patterns on page 30 to make the spine and pockets. Glue the covers to the spine, then glue a pocket between each fold of the spine.

The book made in the project on page 26 is sewn together with ribbon and, to ensure that it opens easily, the cover must have a hinge. To make this hinge, cut a 1cm wide strip off the long edge of the card for the back and front covers. Cut a third strip from a scrap piece of card for use as a template. Draw a line down the middle of this strip, then make five equi-spaced marks along this line – for the project book these are 3cm apart. Punch holes at each mark on the template. Use masking tape or bookbinders' linen to attach the strips to the back and front covers and complete the hinge.

Decorate the cover paper and cut it to size, remembering to include 1cm wide flaps on all sides. Apply spray adhesive to the assembled cover boards, then place these in the centre of the cover paper. Turn in the flaps, glue them to the inside of the cover boards, then glue on the end papers. Use the punched template to mark the bound front and back cover, then punch holes through the covers.

Cut pages (from whatever paper you wish to put inside the book) slightly smaller than the cover. Use the template to mark these, then punch out the holes. Place the pages between the back and front cover and sew the book together with ribbon.

CUTTING APERTURES

When cutting apertures, make a photocopy of the pattern and fix it temporarily to the card with small pieces of low-tack tape. Use a pin or needle tool to pierce through the corners of the pattern and the card. Remove the pattern then, using the pierced points as a guide, cut the aperture with a craft knife and straight edge on a cutting mat.

PAPER PRICKING

This simple, three-hundred-year-old craft gives superb textured effects, especially on Canson Mi-Teintes pastel paper.

The only tool required is a No. 5 sharp sewing needle mounted in a needle vice (this can be bought from lace-making suppliers). Insert the eye of the needle into the vice to leave just 1.5cm of the needle protruding. If the exposed length of needle is too long it may 'whip' and you will not have enough control to make neat perforations. You will also need a perforating mat to prick on; we use a 1cm thick, high-density foam pad, but you could use the foam side of a computer mouse mat.

There are two basic paper pricking techniques: outlining and stippling (filling-in). When outlining a design, you push the needle through the paper to create a series of equal-sized holes, and you can work a design from the front or the back of the paper or a combination of both. When stippling, you just push the tip of the needle through the paper, either from the back or the front of the paper.

The secret of good paper pricking is to create neat rows of equal-sized holes. The size of hole depends on how far you push the needle through the paper: by just breaking through the surface of the paper you get tiny holes; by pushing the needle a little further you get small holes; and by pushing the needle right through you get large holes.

For paper pricking you need to reproduce designs on tracing paper. You can photocopy a given design or you can use the matching rubber stamps and dye ink to create images that complement those on the folding papers. Fix the tracing in position on the front of the card, place the card on the perforating mat, then, keeping the perforations close together, work round the outlines of the design (it does not matter too much if you go slightly off-line). If you want to follow the project design exactly, refer to the photographs of the finished pieces. When you have finished all the perforations on the front of the card, remove the tracing paper, then, without turning it over, fix it to the back of the paper so that it aligns with the pricked design. You can now work the rest of the design.

Filling-in can be worked from either the front or the back of the paper and, as you will be working within a pricked outline, you can dispense with the traced design.

MAKING ENVELOPES

For non-standard-size cards it is easy to make your own envelope. We have included measurements on this pattern, but you can adapt it to make any size of envelope. You can customise plain paper by decorating it with a matching rubber stamp or you can make an envelope out of patterned wallpaper or gift wrap. Some gift wraps are quite flimsy so spray mount these on to thin card before cutting them to shape.

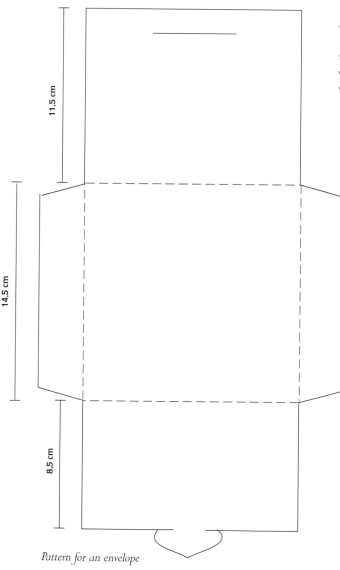

Pattern for an envelope

GOLDEN MUSIC

PHOTOGRAPH ALBUM (See page 15)

Materials
Blank photograph album
4cm folding papers (eighteen)

Method
Fold all eighteen papers to step 9 of fold sequence 1. Slide two folded papers together as steps 10 and 11 to make a double-element fold, then repeat with two more papers. Stick three papers together as shown in the last diagram; make four of these and glue one in each corner of the album. Glue one double-element fold in the middle of each side of the album and the two remaining single-element folds in the middle of the top and bottom of the album.

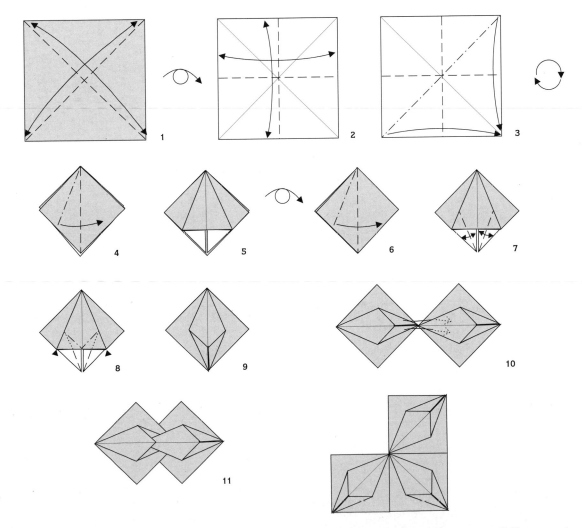

Fold sequence 1

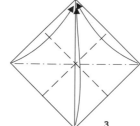

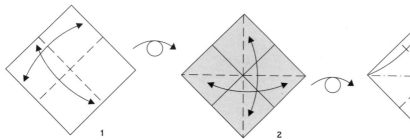

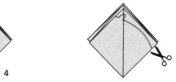

Fold sequence 2

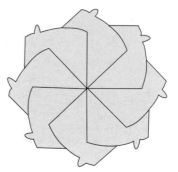

MUSICAL NOTES CARD (See page 15)

Materials
Ochre card (12 x 24cm)
Music paper or sheet music (11cm square)
Green paper (10cm square)
4cm folding papers (eight)

Pattern for Musical Notes Card
Enlarge to 150%

Pattern for the Bass Clef Card
Enlarge to 150%

Method
Fold the ochre-coloured card to form a 12cm square.
Glue the sheet of music in the middle of the card.
Photocopy the pattern above, cut these shapes from the
green paper, then glue them to the music paper. Fold all
eight folding papers to fold sequence 2, then cut them to
shape. Slide and glue the folds together to form a
rosette, then glue this to the card.

Johanna and Hendrik

10th July, 1947

Fold sequence 3

BASS CLEF CARD (See page 15)

Materials
Dark green card (29 x 14.5cm)
Dark green card (6cm square)
Music paper or sheet music (10 x 14cm)
4cm folding papers (eight)

Method
Fold the green card to form a 14.5cm square.
Photocopy the bass clef pattern (see page 14), cut the
shapes from the music paper, then spray glue these on
to the green card. Fold all eight papers to step 9 of fold
sequence 1 (see page 13), then slide them together to
form the rosette shown on fold sequence 3. Glue the
rosette on to the small piece of green card, then cut the
card to a star shape (leaving a narrow green border).
Glue the rosette to the card.

MUSICAL CORNERS CARD (See page 15)

Materials
Dark green card (29 x 14.5cm)
Dark green card (one 10cm and one 10.5cm square)
Music paper (12.5cm square)
4cm folding papers (four)
5cm folding papers (four)

Method
Fold the green card to form a 14.5cm square. Glue the
music paper in the middle of the folded card, then glue
the 10.5cm square of green card on top. Use the
matching rubber stamp and dark green ink to create a
random design on the 10cm square of green paper.
Fold all eight folding papers to fold sequence 4. Slide
and glue one of the 5cm papers over each corner of the
decorated green card, glue the four 4cm papers
together to form the rosette in the middle of the
decorated green card, then, finally, glue this to the plain
green card.

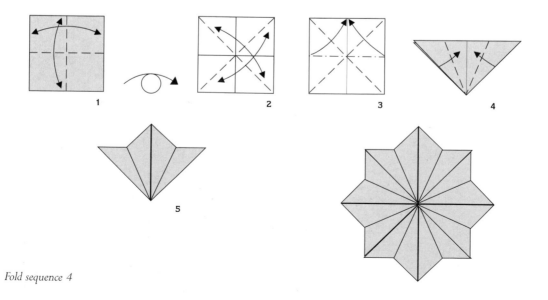

Fold sequence 4

DAISY DAISY

SCALLOPED-EDGE CARD (See page19)

Materials
Dark blue card (26 x 13cm)
White glossy card (12cm square)
4cm folding papers (eight)
Cutting paper

Method
Fold the dark blue paper to form a 13cm square. Using just the flower image of the matching rubber stamp, stamp the glossy white card with colourless embossing ink and embossing powder (see page 8). Lightly sponge the whole of of the card with pale yellow dye ink (see page 8), then cut the edges with fancy-edged scissors. Cut three of the green-with-yellow flower shapes from the cutting paper. Cut one of these in half, then fold and glue each half over two opposite corners of the glossy card. Fold all eight folding papers to step 4 of fold sequence 2 (see page 14), then cut round the shape of the flowers. Slide and glue the papers together to form a rosette. Cut one of the dark blue shapes from the cutting paper, then glue the rosette to it. Layer the rosette with the other two shapes from the cutting paper on to the glossy card, then glue this to the blue card.

SKEWED-CENTRE CARD (See page19)

Materials
Dark blue card (26 x 13cm)
White glossy card (10cm square)
4cm folding papers (seven)
Cutting paper

Method
Fold the dark blue card to form a 13cm square, then stamp it using just the flower image of the matching rubber stamp and dark blue dye ink. Stamp the glossy card as described for the previous project. Cut one of the green-with-yellow flowers designs from the cutting paper, cut this into quarters, then stick one of these to each corner of the glossy card. Fold six folding papers to fold sequence 5, then slide and glue them together to make the rosette. Cut the centre of the flower from the last folding paper, then secure this in the middle of the rosette with a spot of silicone glue or a self-adhesive tab. Glue the rosette to the centre of the glossy card, then glue this at a skewed angle on to the dark blue card.

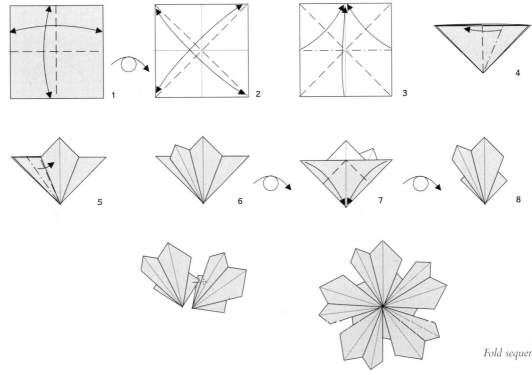

Fold sequence 5

LAYERED CARD (See page 19)

Materials
Dark blue card (28 x 14cm)
4cm folding papers (four)
Cutting paper
Folding paper (12cm square)

Method
Fold the dark blue card to form a 14cm square, then use the matching stamp and dark blue dye ink to create a random design. From the cutting sheet cut out one large blue design with green centre, one large design depicting the flower edges, the small yellow design and the plain orange design. Layer and glue these so that the points of each shape are between the points of the image below. Cut the four folding papers in half diagonally, then fold all eight half papers to fold sequence 6. Slide and glue them together, then make the last folds to complete the rosette. Glue the rosette on to the layered cutting papers. Cut a 10cm square aperture in the 12cm square piece of folding paper to form a border. Glue the border to the dark blue card then, finally, glue on the completed rosette.

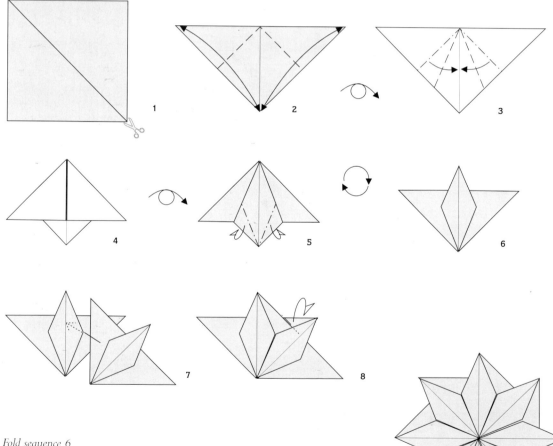

Fold sequence 6

TRANSPARENT FRAME (See page 19)

Materials
Transparent plastic frame (15 x 20cm)
4cm folding papers (two)
Concentric-circle paper (two sheets)
Gold sequins (eight)
Cutting paper (four sheets, from which you must cut
two of the orange with yellow centre designs and four
of the large designs with flowers on a blue background.

Method
This project uses segments of the folding and cutting
paper designs to create a symmetrical design. The
design is assembled on the concentric-circle paper which
is then cut to waste. Only apply glue to the middle of
each of the inner segments, and to just the tip of each of
the outer ones.

　　Glue a 4cm folding paper to the middle of the circle,
aligning its corners to the spokes of the circle. Cut the
orange/yellow cutting paper into eight segments and
glue these on the folding paper as shown below,
aligning the points with the spokes of the circle. Cut
each of the two large blue designs into eight segments
(see photograph on page 19). Glue eight of these
segments on to the circle paper, aligning them to the
flower centre of first layer. Glue the tips of the last
eight segments and align them with the flower centres
on the previous set of segments. Carefully cut away the
remains of the circle paper so that none of it shows.
Repeat these instructions to make the second design (if
required), then glue them together back to back. Use
tiny spots of clear-drying glue to mount the design on
the clear plastic, and to secure the gold sequins round
the design, then assemble the frame.

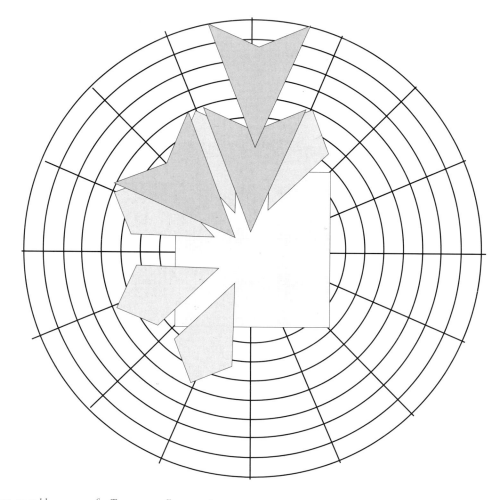

Segment assembly sequence for Transparent Frame project

CHINESE PEONY

FLOWERS CARD (See page 23)

Materials
Dark blue card (26 x 13cm)
Lilac card (11.5 x 6cm)
5cm folding papers (eight)

Method
Fold the dark blue card to form a 13cm square. Draw a 10.5cm diameter semicircle, centred on the long edge of the lilac card, then carefully cut it out. Use a fancy punch to cut out flowers round the semicircle (see page 10). Referring to the photograph on page 23, glue the semicircle and the other part of of the lilac paper to the dark blue card, then add three of the punched flower shapes. Fold all eight papers to fold sequence 7 (cutting round the flower shapes), glue them together, then glue the rosette to the card.

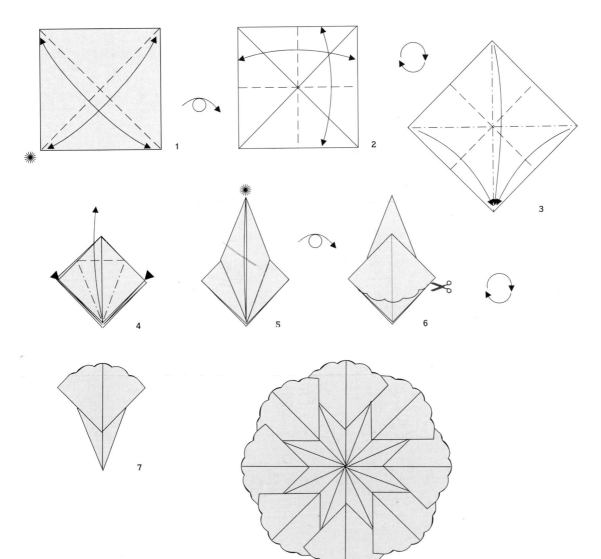

Fold sequence 7

LAYERED CARD (See page 23)

Materials
Dark blue card (26 x 13cm)
Lilac card (one 10cm and one 8cm square)
Dark blue card (one 9cm and one 7cm square)
5cm folding papers (eight)
4cm folding papers (four)

Method
Fold the large piece of dark blue paper to form a 13cm square. Glue the four smaller pieces of card on top of each other rotating each one-quarter-turn, then glue these to the folded card. Glue one of the 4cm folding papers to the centre of the layered card. Fold all eight 5cm folding papers to fold sequence 8, slide and glue them together, then glue the rosette on to the card. Referring to the project on page 25, cut the other three 4cm folding papers to create the three smallest shapes, then use blobs of silicone glue to fix these in the centre of the rosette.

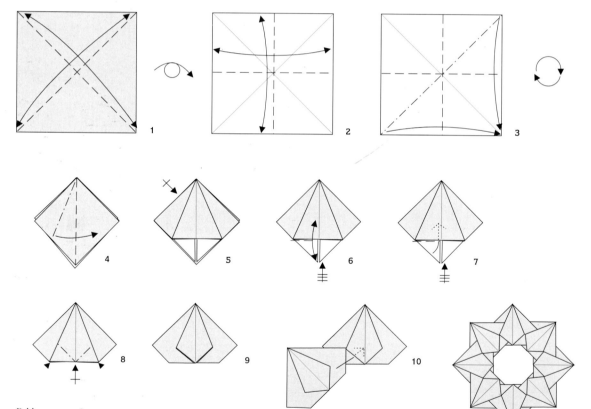

Fold sequence 8

STAR CARD (See page 23)

Materials
Lilac card (26 x 13cm)
Lilac card (offcut)
Dark blue card (9cm square)
5cm folding papers (eight)

Note: The 5cm folding papers must be cut in a special way to achieve the full peony shape in the middle of the star rosette. Each must be cut from the middle of a block of four 5cm folding papers, using the flower centres as the corners of each piece. You can cut three 5cm papers out of one sheet of folding papers.

Method
Fold the large lilac card in half to form a 13cm square. Referring to the photograph on page 23, punch a row of holes along the top and right-hand edges of the dark blue card. Cut two narrow strips from the lilac card, weave these through the punched holes, then glue the blue card to the lilac card. Fold all eight folding papers to step 6 of fold sequence 9. Slide and glue them together to form the rosette, then glue this to the corner of the card.

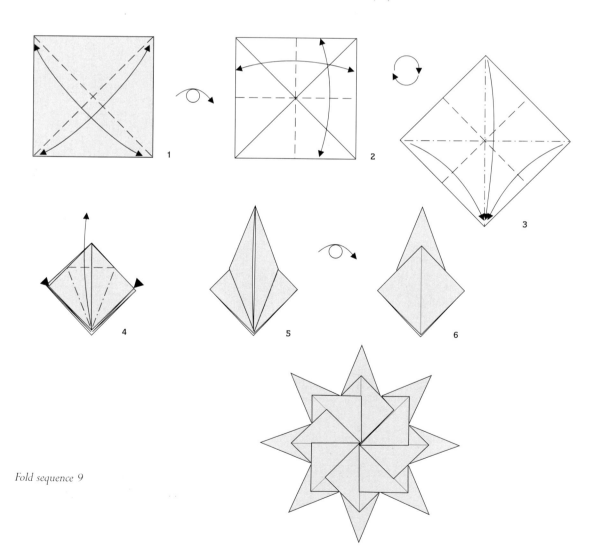

Fold sequence 9

STAR BOX (See front cover)

Materials
Glossy white card (30 x 20cm)
3mm thick foam board or mountboard (10 x 20cm)
5cm folding paper (one)
4cm folding papers (five)
Cutting paper

Method
Use just the flower area of a matching stamp, with colourless embossing ink and embossing powder, to create a random design on the glossy white card (see page 8). Sponge the whole of the card with pale and dark pink dye ink. Sponge the back of the card, then randomly stamp it with dark blue dye ink. Cut a 6cm wide by 28.5cm long strip from the decorated glossy card for the sides of the base of the box, then score folds, 17.5mm apart, across it. Cut another strip, 2cm wide by 29.3cm long, for the sides of the lid and score folds, 18mm apart, across it. Each strip has a 0.5cm flap at one end to make the join.

Using the patterns below cut the base and lid from the 3mm thick foam board, then make up the box (see page 11). Glue the 5cm folding paper to the top of the lid. Cut a peony star shape from the cutting paper, then glue this on top of the folding paper. Cut the fives shapes given below from the 4cm folding papers, then using silicone glue or small self-adhesive pads, build a three-dimensional flower head.

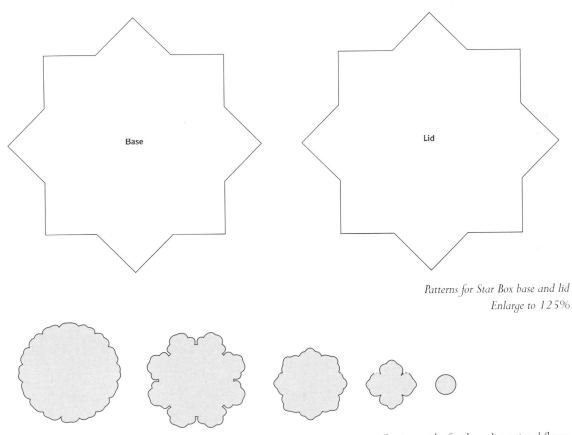

Base

Lid

Patterns for Star Box base and lid
Enlarge to 125%

Cutting guides for three-dimensional flower.
Cut each shape from one folding paper

NOTE BOOK (see page 23)

Materials
1mm thick card (two 10.5 x 15cm rectangles)
Dark blue paper (to cover the cards)
White paper (for the pages of the book)
Thin ribbon
4cm folding papers (seven)

Method
Use the matching rubber stamp and white pigment ink to create a random design on the dark blue paper. Leave this to dry for at least one hour, then make up the book (see page 11). Cut the folding papers in half, then fold all fourteen of these half-papers to fold sequence 10. Assemble and glue these together to create a border on the front cover of the book.

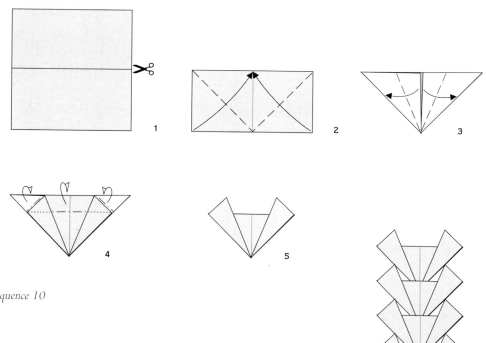

Fold sequence 10

MUSIC BLUES

RIBBON CARD (See front cover)

Materials
White glossy card (26 x 13cm)
White glossy card (11cm square)
Dark blue card (12cm square)
4cm folding papers (twelve)
Pale blue organza ribbon (4cm wide)
Silver wire

Method
Fold the large white glossy paper to form a 13cm square. Sponge pale blue dye ink on the 11cm square of white glossy card. Use decorative corner scissors to cut the fancy corners on all cards. Photocopy the aperture pattern, then cut this out of the front of the folded card and the middle of the other two cards. Glue the dark blue card to the folded card, aligning the apertures. Weave the ribbon on the back of the sponged card (see page 9), then glue this card to the dark blue card. Glue two of the folding papers together back to back. When this is dry, cut its corners with the corner punch, then stick this shape between the two layers of ribbon. Fold the remaining ten 4cm folding papers to step 4 of fold sequence 11, then glue two sets of five folds together as part-rosettes. Stick these to the top left-hand corner and bottom right-hand corner of the card. Use patterns (right) and silver wire to make the three musical notes (see page 10), then glue them on the card.

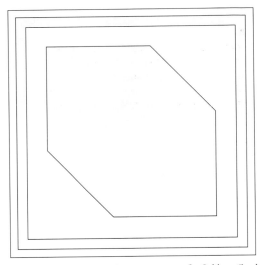

Aperture pattern for Ribbon Card
Enlarge to 200%

Use the silver wire to make these musical notes

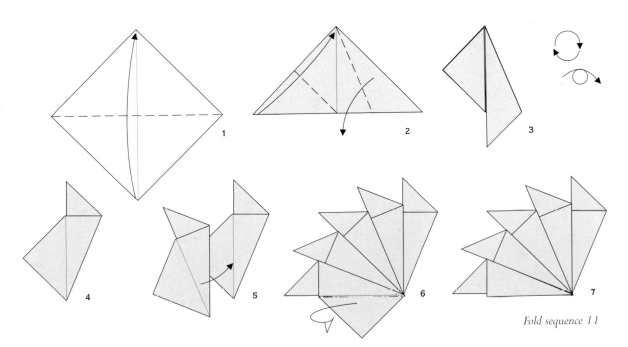

Fold sequence 11

TREBLE CLEF CARD (see page 31)

Materials
Dark blue card (27.5 x 17.5cm)
Dark blue card (9cm square)
5cm folding papers (five)
Folding paper
Cutting paper

Method
Fold the large piece of dark blue card so that the front is 13cm wide. Cut a 1cm strip of folding paper, then glue this to the inside back of the card, aligning it with the front edge of the card. Use fancy-edged scissors to cut along the right-hand side of the strip. Photocopy the treble clef pattern, cut this out of the folding paper, then glue it to the card. Cut the 5cm folding papers in half, then fold all ten half-papers to fold sequence 13. Cut a pale blue shape and one of the shapes that has music notes round its edge from the cutting paper. Glue the pale blue shape to the square of dark blue card then, alternating the points, glue the other shape on top. Cut the blue card to leave a narrow border all round. Glue the rosette in the centre, then glue this on the card.

Pattern for the Treble Clef Card
Enlarge to 150%

CHECKERBOARD CARD (see page 31)

Materials:
Dark blue card (28 x 14cm folded)
4cm folding papers (thirteen)
Silver metal sheet (11cm square)

Method
Fold the card to form a 14cm square. Transfer the pattern for the checkerboard on to the metal, emboss it (see page 10), then glue it on to the card. Fold all papers to fold sequence 24 (see page 49), then glue these on to the blank squares of the checkerboard.

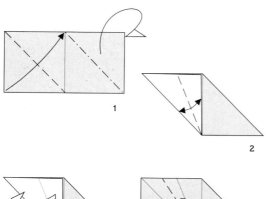

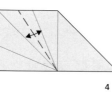

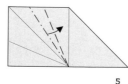

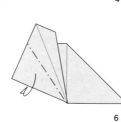

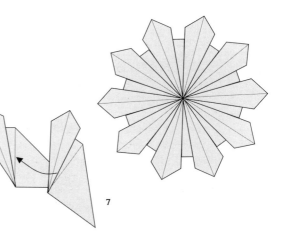

Fold sequence 13

Pattern for Checkerboard Card. Enlarge to 150%

the back of the rosette, placing one between each of the points as shown on the pattern. Use small blobs of silicone glue to build up the three-dimensional rosette, layering the two small silver stars, the two plain blue shapes and the small music design shape, then glue the rosette on to the card.

PLASTIC MEDALLION (see page 31)

The rosette is made in much the same way as the metal one above, but use just the central rosette with an additional plain blue shape and a slightly larger metal star shape (with stippled edges) which goes at the back. Make two rosettes, glue them back to back, then place into a plastic medallion.

METAL ROSETTE (see page 31)

Materials
Dark blue card (30 x 18cm)
Dark blue card (21 x 15cm)
Cutting paper
Silver metal sheet (30 x 21cm)

Method
Use the matching stamp and dark blue dye ink to create a random design on the large piece of dark blue card, then fold it to form a 15 x 18cm rectangle. Photocopy the pattern, then use this as a guide to cut star shapes from the small piece of dark blue card and the metal sheet (cut two small metal star shapes). Use the stippling technique to add texture to the edges of the large and medium sized metal stars (see page 10). Cut one small and one large music design shape, and two dark blue shapes from the cutting paper. Prepare the two dark blue shapes and the small music design shape for faux fold rosettes (see page 7). Prepare the two small silver stars in a similar way, by embossing lines between opposite points and making cuts between the valleys. Referring to the pattern, make up the outer rosette starting with the largest of the silver stars, then layering the large dark blue star, the medium size silver star and the small dark blue star. Cut the large music design shape into eight segments, then glue these to

Silver metal sheet

Dark blue card

Musical design shapes from cutting paper

Pattern for the Metal Rosette project. Enlarge to 150%

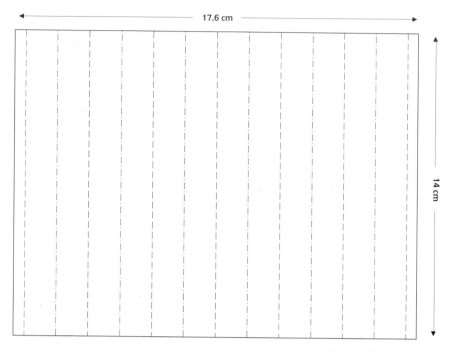

17,6 cm

14 cm

Pattern for the spine of the CD Holder
Enlarge to 200%

CD HOLDER (See page 31)

Materials

2mm thick card (two, 14cm squares)
Glossy white card (two, 16cm squares)
Dark blue paper (18 x 14cm)
Folding paper or sheet music (size to suit pockets)

Folding paper (two, 13.5cm square)
4cm folding papers (eight)
5cm folding papers (eight)

continued on page 32.

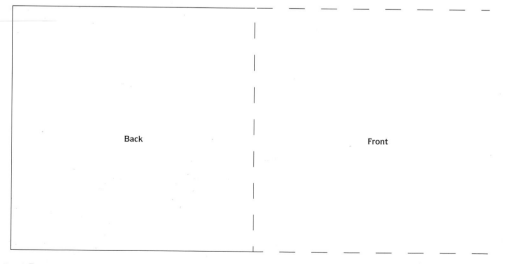

Back

Front

Pattern for the pockets of the CD Holder
Enlarge to 200%

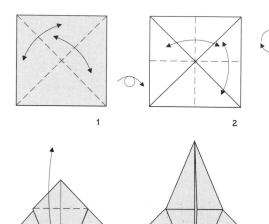

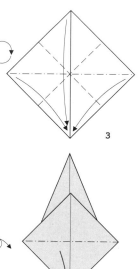

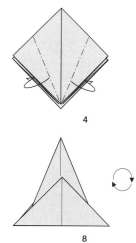

Fold sequence 14

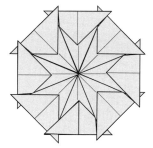

Method

Use the matching rubber stamp with clear embossing ink and embossing powder to create a random pattern on the glossy card. Sponge the whole sheet with pale and dark blue dye ink. Make the book as described on page 11, using the stamped glossy paper for covering the front and back covers, the dark blue paper for the spine, the sheet music for the pockets and the squares of folding paper for the end papers. Fold the 4cm folding papers to fold sequence 14, then glue the rosette to the middle of the front cover. Fold the 5cm folding papers to fold sequence 15, then glue these to the corners of the front cover.

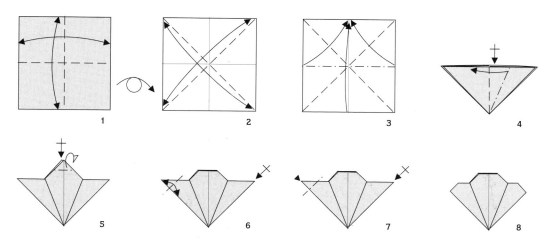

Fold sequence 15

AUTUMN LEAVES

PAPER-PRICKED CARD (See page 52)

Materials
Rust card (28 x 14cm)
Ivory paper (10.5cm square)
4cm folding papers (eight)

Method
Fold the rust card to form a 14cm square. Fold 4cm folding papers to fold sequence 16 (cut out the top of the leaf shapes as shown at step 2, then slide and glue the folds together to form the rosette. Trim the edges of the ivory paper with fancy-edged scissors, or use the photograph as a guide to perforate a design. Use the matching stamp and the paper pricking technique (see page 11) to prick four leaves in the corners of the ivory paper, glue this to the base card, then glue on the rosette.

TRIANGULAR BOOK (See page 35)

Materials
2mm thick card (13cm x 22cm)
Rust card (A4 sheet)
Cream paper for the pages
Cutting paper (Falling leaves design)
Copper metal sheet (7 x 12cm)
Folding paper (Autumn leaves design)

Method
Photocopy the patterns on page 34, then cut two book covers from the 2mm thick card. Use just the leaf shape on the matching rubber stamp and sepia dye ink to create a random pattern on the rust card, then use the pattern to cut the triangles with flaps. Glue these to the cover boards, turning the flaps over on to the back of the covers. Cut two triangles from the Autumn Leaves

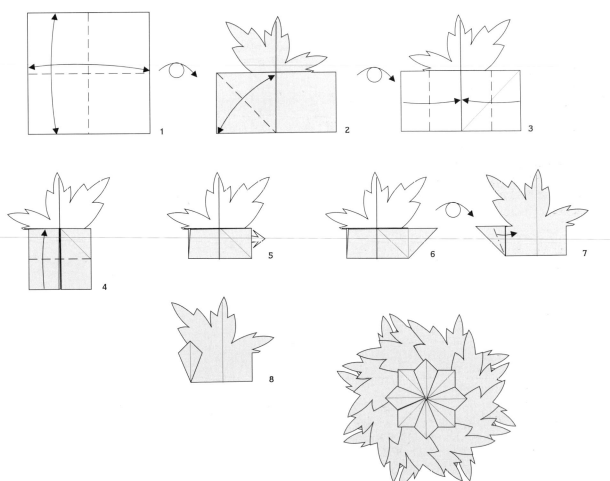

Fold sequence 16

2mm thick card

Folding paper

Copper coloured
metal sheet

Rust coloured paper

Patterns for the covers of the Triangular Book project
Enlarge to 200%

folding paper, then glue them in the middle of the the book covers. Cut two 7cm triangles from the copper metal and use the matching stamp to emboss a leaf in the centre of each one (see page 10). Emboss round the edges of the metal triangles, either by making a series of freehand dots or by using a plastic quilting wheel and a ruler. Glue the metal on to the book covers. Use the pattern below to cut out a set of pages. If you want more pages, cut another set, then, making sure you get

them the correct way round, glue the two ends together. Fold the pages and glue the first and last page to the back of the covers as end papers. If you want to personalise your book, you can decorate the pages of it by sponging and stamping, by applying small folded designs or cutting-paper rosettes, or by mounting pressed flowers, leaves, photographs, or pieces of verse on them.

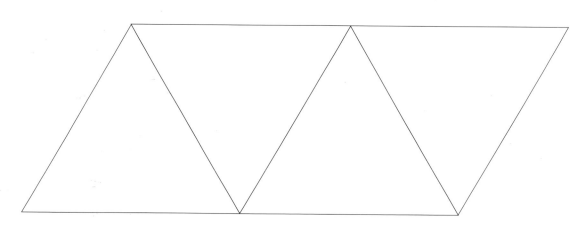

Pattern for the pages of the Triangular Book project
Enlarge to 200%

RIBBON WEAVING CARD (See page 52)

Materials
Cream card (30 x 15cm)
Cream card (15cm square)
Camel organza ribbon
Gold metal sheet
4cm folding papers (eight)
5cm folding papers (eight)

Method
Use a matching stamp and beige dye ink to create a
random design on the large piece of cream card, then
fold it to form a 15cm square. Cut four 5cm square
apertures in the middle of the front of the card, leaving
a 1.5cm strip between each aperture. Cut the same
apertures on the 15cm square of cream card (the
weaving frame), then trim 0.5cm off each edge of this
card. Weave the ribbons over the apertures on the
frame (see page 9), then glue the frame to the inside
front of the folded card. Cut a few small leaf shapes
from the metal sheet and glue these between the layers
of ribbon. Cut out two larger leaves, emboss their veins,
then glue one to the top left-hand corner and one to the
bottom right-hand corner of the card. Ensuring that the
folding papers are all the same way round, fold the 5cm
papers to fold sequence 2 (see page 14), cutting round
the edges of the leaves. Glue this leaf rosette to the
card. Now use the 4cm papers in the same way to make
a smaller leaf rosette and glue this to the card to finish
the project.

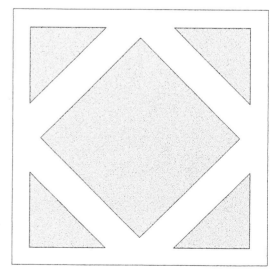

Pattern for the Aperture Card on page 37
Enlarge to 200%

HARVEST QUILT

APERTURE CARD (See page 38)

Materials
Dark green card (29 x 14.5cm)
Pale green card (14cm square)
4cm folding papers (four)
5cm folding papers (four)

Method
Fold the dark green card to form a 14.5cm square. Fold the four 5cm folding papers to fold sequence 17 (see page 39), then slide and glue them together to create a rosette. Fold the 4cm folding papers in the same way but only to step 7. Using the pattern on page 36 as a guide, cut out the apertures on the front of the folded card, then glue the pale green card behind. Glue the 5cm rosette on the centre aperture and a 4cm fold on each corner.

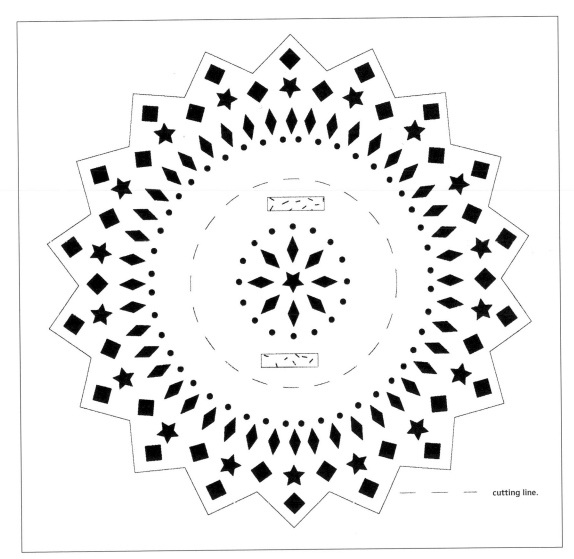

— — — — **cutting line.**

Pattern for the Paper Lace Card 1 on page 40

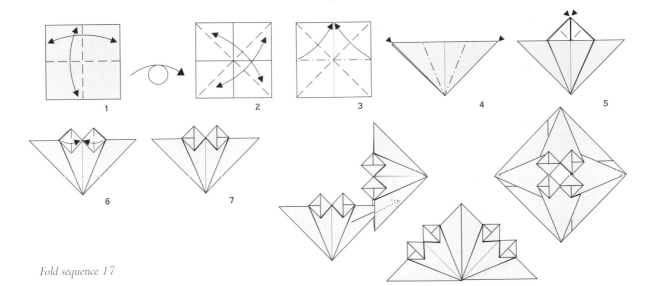

Fold sequence 17

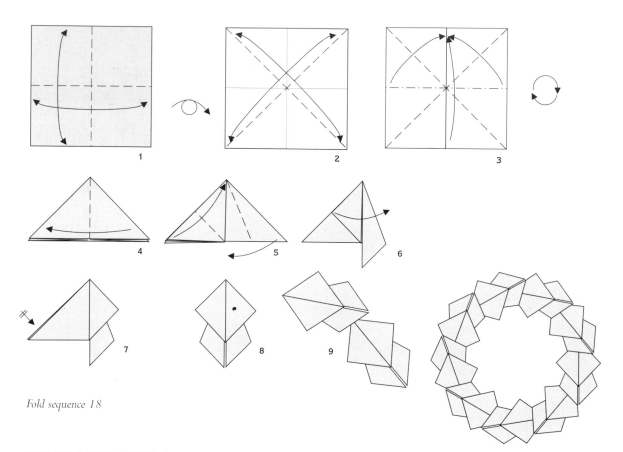

Fold sequence 18

PAPER LACE CARD 1 (See page 38)

Materials
Cream card (30 x 15cm)
Dark green paper (15cm square)
4cm folding papers (thirteen)

Method
Sponge the cream card lightly with purple dye ink, fold
the card to form a 15cm square, then cut the corners
with decorative corner scissors. Fold four of the 4cm
folding papers diagonally, glue the fold, then glue each
triangle in a corner on the back of the card. Photocopy
the pattern (see page 37) then, using small spots of
rubber solution adhesive placed between the central
design and the dashed circle, attach it to the dark green
paper. Cut the dark green paper to the star shape, then
use fancy paper punches to cut out the shapes between
the outer edge and the dashed circle. Use a craft knife
to make a short slit in the dashed circle then, working
carefully, use scissors to cut round the rest of the circle
and remove the centre area of the design. Now punch
out the shapes in the central area. Glue the large piece
of paper lace centrally on to the card front, then glue
the small piece in the centre. Fold the remaining nine

4cm folding papers to fold sequence 18 and create a
wreath, then glue this on to the paper lace so that it
covers up the join.

PAPER LACE CARD 2 (See page 38)

Materials
Burgundy card (29 x 14.5cm)
Dark green paper (8cm square)
Matching gift wrap (14.5cm square)
4cm folding papers (four)
Cutting paper

Method
Cut the folding papers in half, then fold the eight half-
papers to fold sequence 19. Cut a large green shape
and a patterned piece from the cutting paper. Glue the
patterned piece on top of the green shape, placing the
points of one between those of the other. Glue the folds
on top, aligning their points with those on the green

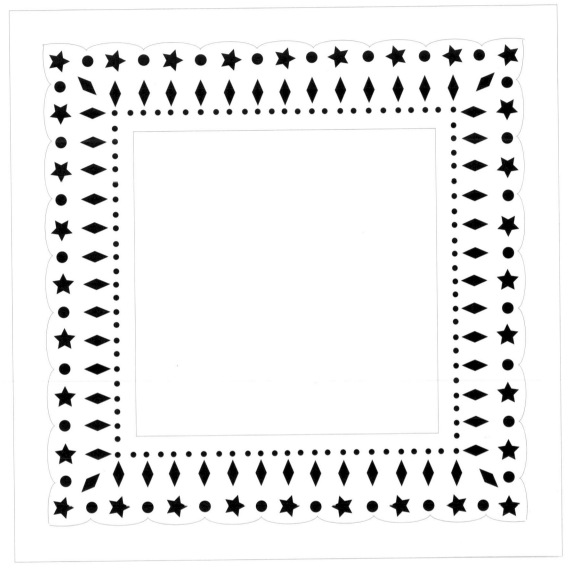

Pattern for the Paper Lace Card 2

shape. Photocopy the pattern above, attach it to the gift wrap and make the lace design as described in the previous project; punch the inner, small circles first, then work outwards. Fold the burgundy card to form a 14.5cm square, then glue on the paper lace, the piece of dark green card and, finally, the completed rosette.

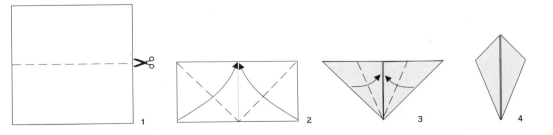

Fold sequence 19

ADDRESS BOOK (See page 39)

Materials
Hardback address book (15.5 x 21.5cm)
Dark green paper (37 x 26cm)
Pale green paper (A4 sheet)
Clear, thin acetate (A4 sheet)
Matching paper for the end papers (two, A4 sheets)
5cm folding papers (eight)
Folding paper
Cutting paper

Note: The pattern below is sized to suit the dimensions of the book used for this project. If your book has different dimensions, adjust the pattern to suit. The critical measurements are those for the apertures, which are sized to match those of the finished folds.

Method
Use a matching rubber stamp and dark green dye ink to create a pattern on the green paper, then, referring to the pattern below, cut out the apertures. Place the pale green paper under the apertures and mark their shapes on to it. Glue the sheet of acetate behind the apertures in the dark green paper.

Fold all eight 5cm papers to fold sequence 17 (see page 39). Glue pairs of these, side by side, on each corner area marked on the pale green paper. Cut a 10cm square from the folding paper, then cut a 7.5cm square from the middle of this to create a border. Glue this border in the middle area marked on the pale green paper. Cut out one pale lilac, one dark lilac, one pale green and one patterned shape from the cutting sheet, then, with each layer slightly skewed, make up a rosette (see page 7). Glue the rosette in the centre of the border on the pale green paper. Glue the pale green paper behind the apertures of the dark green paper matching the apertures up carefully. Cover the address book, turning in the flaps and gluing them on the inside covers. Cut the matching end papers approximately 0.5cm smaller than the inside covers then glue them over the flaps to give a neat finish.

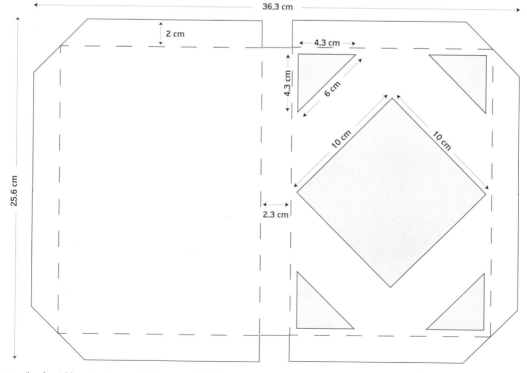

Pattern for the Address Book cover. Enlarge to 200%

BUTTERFLY DAWN

LACE PAPER CARD (See page 46)

Materials
Pale blue card (28 x 14cm)
Dark blue card (two, 12cm squares)
Lace paper (11cm square)
Gold sequins (sixteen)
4cm folding papers (eight)
Cutting paper

Method
Fold the pale blue card to form a 14cm square, cut a 9cm square aperture in the middle of the front of the folded card, then glue the lace paper over this. Cut a 9cm square aperture in the middle of both pieces of dark blue card. Glue one of these to the inside front of the card matching up the apertures precisely. Starting at one corner, punch small holes at regular intervals round the other blue card. Glue this to the front of the card, matching up the apertures carefully, then glue the sequins over each of the holes. Cut two dark blue shapes and two of the pale blue with gold centre shapes from the cutting paper. Glue one of the pale blue shapes on to a dark blue shape so that the points of one are between the points of the other. Repeat with the other two shapes. Fold the 4cm folding papers to fold sequence 20, then glue them together on one of assembled cut-out shapes. Glue the finished rosette in the middle of the lace paper. Glue the other two prepared shapes on the inside of the card to cover the back of the rosette.

BOX (See page 47)

Materials
Corrugated box (10cm diameter)
4cm folding papers (twenty-one)

Note: If you cannot find a box with corrugated sides, you can use strips of corrugated paper to cover the sides of a plain box (see page 11).

Method
Sponge the inside and outside of the box with light blue acrylic paint. When the paint is dry, use a gold gel pen to colour the lines between the corrugations. Fold the 4cm folding papers to fold sequence 22 (see page 45), cut them to shape, glue them together to form the rosette, then glue this to the top of the box.

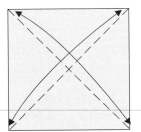

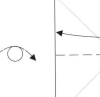
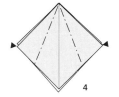
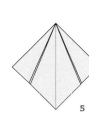
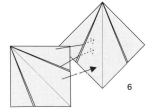
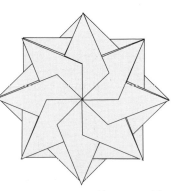

Fold sequence 20

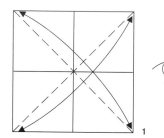

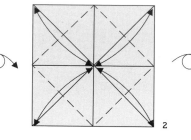

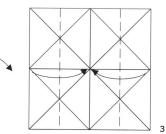

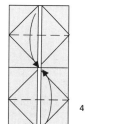

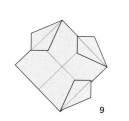

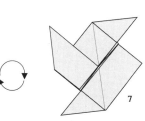

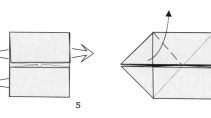

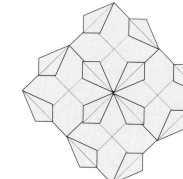

Fold sequence 21

WINDOW CARD (See page 46)

Materials
Pale blue card (29 x 14.5cm)
Pale blue card (10cm square)
Clear acetate (9cm square)
5cm folding papers (eight)
Folding paper

Method
Use a matching rubber stamp and pale blue dye ink to create a random design on the large piece of pale blue card. Fold the card to form a 14.5cm square, then cut an 8cm square aperture diagonally on the front of the card. Cut the same aperture in the other piece of card to make a frame. Glue the acetate to the inside front cover, then glue the pale blue frame on top of it to give a neat finish. Cut a 10cm square from the folding paper, then cut an 8cm square from the middle of this to form a border. Glue this border on the front of the

card. Fold the 5cm folding papers to fold sequence 21, making two shapes from four folds. Glue one finished shape to each side of the acetate aperture.

PARCHMENT PICTURE (See page 46)

Materials
2mm thick card (two, 17cm squares)
Parchment paper or vellum (17cm square)
4cm folding papers (four)
Cutting paper

Method
Cut a 13cm square aperture from one of the pieces of card to make a frame. Sponge and stamp both pieces of card with pale blue and a little dark blue dye ink and

continued on page 48.

Fold sequence 22

Lace perforations pattern for Parchment Picture project

Embossing pattern for Parchment Picture project

☀ = 2 estralina (star) tools, large and
small. Alternatively you can
emboss dots.

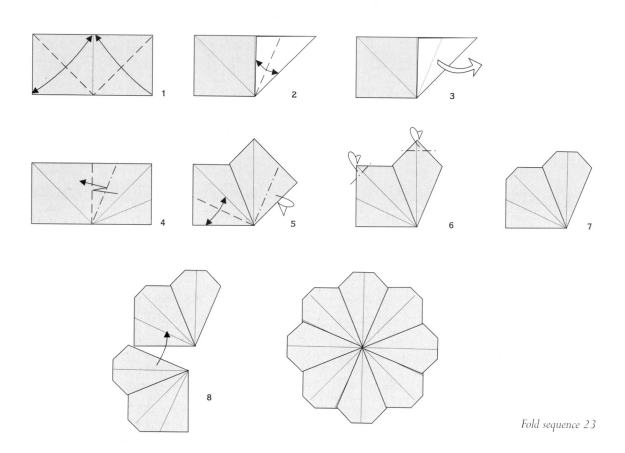

Fold sequence 23

gold pigment ink. Use small pieces of masking tape to fix the parchment paper to a perforating grid, then use a needle tool (or the paper-pricking needle) to perforate the lace pattern shown on page 45 (each square on the pattern represents a hole on the grid; only perforate the squares marked with a dot). This design requires a 13cm square lace area, so you will have to extend the pattern. Remove the lace from the grid, then emboss the design given on the other diagram. Referring to the photograph on page 46, cut the perforations to large crosses. Trim the parchment paper to a 15cm square, glue it behind the frame, then glue the frame on top of the other card. Cut a large dark blue shape and a small pale blue shape from the cutting sheet, then glue these one on top of the other. Fold the 4cm folding papers to fold sequence 23, glue them together to form the rosette, then glue this to the cutting papers. Finally, glue the finished rosette in the middle of the parchment paper.

CIRCULAR PANEL (See page 47)

Materials
2mm thick card (two, 30cm squares)
Folding sheet
Cutting sheet (three)
Concentric-circle paper

Note: Refer to page 20 for gluing instructions for the component parts of this type of design.

Method
Cut a 25cm square aperture in the middle of one of the pieces of card to make a frame. Sponge the frame with pale blue dye ink and a little gold pigment ink then, using a crackle stamp and dark blue dye ink and gold pigment ink, stamp a random design on top. Sponge the backboard (the other piece of card) with pale blue and pale yellow dye ink, then make light, radiating smears of gold pigment ink. Powder the whole backboard with a little sparkle-gold pearl-ex pigment powder (brush it on and off). Leave the coloured pieces

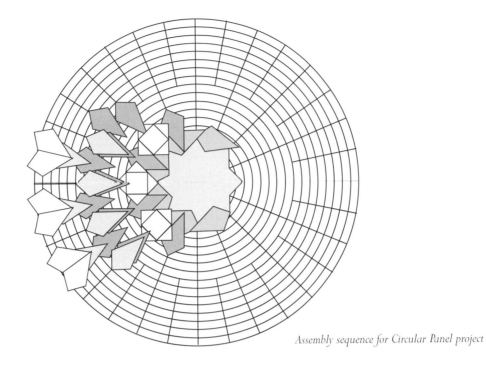

Assembly sequence for Circular Panel project

to dry, preferably overnight. Cut a butterfly design from the cutting paper, glue this to the middle of the circle paper then, referring to the assembly sequence above, build up the circular design from the middle outwards.

(1) Blue with pale centre cutting paper (8 segments)
(2) Dark blue cutting paper (8 segments)
(3) 4cm papers to fold sequence 24 (8 folds)
(4) Pale blue with gold cutting paper (16 segments)

(5) Butterfly design cutting paper (16 segments)
(6) Dark blue cutting paper (16 segments).
(7) Blue with pale centre cutting paper (16 segments)
(8) 4cm half-papers to step 5 of fold sequence 23, then fold back the bottom left-hand corner (16 folds)

When you have finished the assembly, cut the circle paper to waste, glue the design to the middle of the backboard, then glue the frame to the backboard.

Fold sequence 24

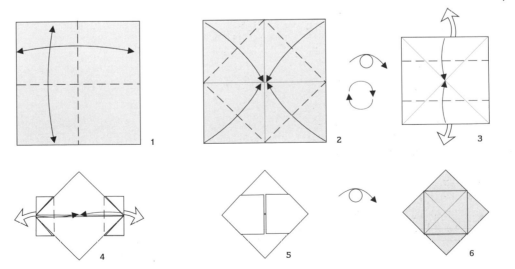

FALLING LEAVES

TILE CARD (See page 52)

Materials
Rust card (24 x 12cm)
Cream card (11cm square)
4cm folding papers (eight)
5cm folding paper (one)
2mm thick white card (6cm square)

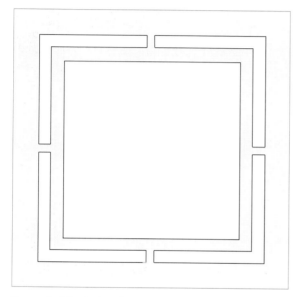

Pattern for Tile Card. Enlarge to 150%

Method
Fold the rust card to form a 12cm square. Photocopy the pattern, cut the cream card to shape, then glue this on to the rust card. Glue the 5cm folding paper flat on the white card, then trim the card to leave a narrow border. Smear the top of this tile with clear embossing ink and emboss it with two or three layers of clear, ultra-thick embossing enamel or three or four layers of ordinary, clear embossing powder. Glue the tile diagonally in the middle of the card. Fold the 4cm folding papers to fold sequence 25, then glue pairs of these together in the corners of the card.

RECTANGULAR CARD (See page 52)

Materials
Cream card (20 x 12.5cm)
Rust card (4 x 18cm)
4cm folding papers (six)

Method
Fold the cream card to form a 10 x 12.5cm rectangle. Use fancy-edged scissors to cut two narrow strips from the rust paper, then glue these diagonally across the folded card. Use the matching rubber stamp and dark brown dye ink to stamp a few leaves in the top left-hand corner of the card. Fold the 4cm folding papers to fold sequence 26 (see page 51), assemble the rosette then glue this to the corner of the card.

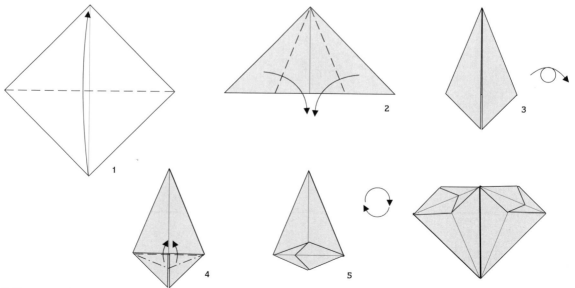

Fold sequence 25

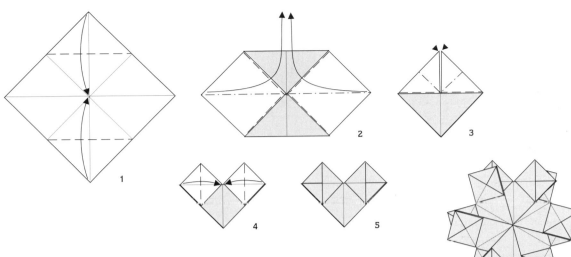

Fold sequence 26

ZIGZAG CARD (See page 52)

Materials required:
Rust card (21 x 15cm)
Cream card (15 x 8cm)
4cm folding papers (six)

Method
Fold the rust card to form a rectangle 10.5 x 15cm. Cut three 4.5cm squares and one 3.5 x 15cm strip from the cream card. Use a gold gel pen to make dashed lines along the edges of the three squares, then, overlapping them slightly, glue these diagonally just short of the front edge of the rust card. Cut the front edge of the card, following the zigzag shape of the three squares, to leave a narrow rust border. Glue the strip of cream card to the inside back page of the card, then use the gold pen to make more dashed lines. Fold three 4cm folding papers to step 5 of fold sequence 26, and three to step 3 of fold sequence 9 (see page 24). Glue one of each fold together (see below), then glue each of these on a cream square.

DIAMOND CARD 1 (See page 52)

Materials
Rust card (30 x 15cm)
Rust card (two, 4.5cm squares)
Cream paper (11.5cm square)
Cream paper (15cm square)
4cm folding papers (four)
Cutting paper (Falling Leaves design)
Cutting paper (Autumn Leaves design)
Gold origami paper

Method
Fold the large piece of rust card to form a 15cm square. Cut the two rust squares diagonally in half, then glue these triangles 0.5cm in from the corners of the cream square. Cut out two of the leaves shapes from the Falling Leaves cutting paper, glue one each under opposite corners of the 11.5cm cream square, then glue the cream paper to the middle of the rust card. Use the matching rubber stamp and sepia dye ink

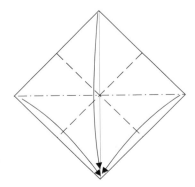

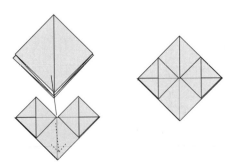

Fold assembly for Zigzag Card

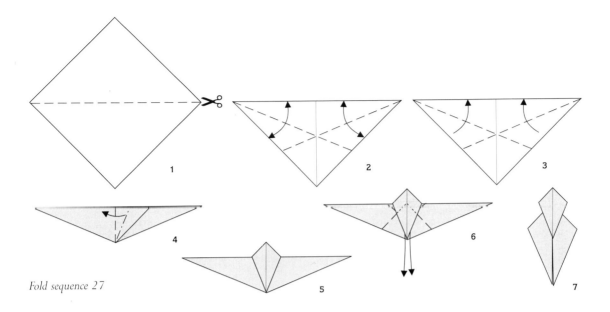

Fold sequence 27

to stamp four images on to the 15cm square of cream paper and two images on the back of the gold origami paper, then cut them all to star shapes. Prepare these for faux fold rosettes (see page 7). Cut out the large leaves shape from the Autumn Leaves cutting paper, glue this to the middle of the card, then glue alternate layers of stamped cream and gold papers, with the points of one between the points on the layer underneath. Finally, cut two more leaves shapes from the Falling Leaves cutting sheet, then glue these on top of the three-dimensional rosette. Fold the 4cm folding papers to fold sequence 27, then glue these on to the corners.

DIAMOND CARD 2 (See page 51)

Materials
Rust card (30 x 15cm)
Rust card (two, 5cm squares)
Cream paper (12.5cm square)
4cm folding papers (eight)
5cm folding paper (four)

Method
Make the basic card in the same way as for the previous project. Fold four of the 4cm folding papers to fold sequence 27, then glue these to the rust corners. Fold the other four 4cm and the four 5cm folding papers to fold sequence 28, then slide all eight folds together to form a rosette. Glue the rosette in the middle of the card.

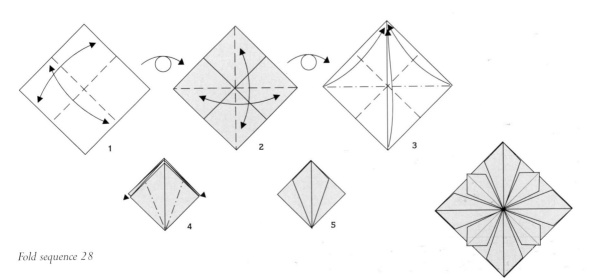

Fold sequence 28

BOX (See page 35)

Materials
White glossy card (A4 sheet)
Rust card (6.3cm square)
4cm folding papers (six)
Clear acetate (6.5cm square)
Gold coloured metal sheet

Method
Use just the leaf part of the Autumn Leaf rubber stamp and gold pigment ink to create a random design on the glossy card, then emboss it with clear embossing powder. Sponge all the card with beige and sepia ink with touches of purple dye ink. Sponge the back of the card in the same way, stamp a random design using plum and sepia dye ink. Photocopy the pattern below, then use this to cut the shapes of the box and its lid from the glossy card.

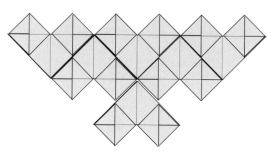

Fold assembly for Box project

Cut the triangular aperture in the lid and in the square of rust card. Make up the box (see page 11). Glue the acetate to the rust card, then trim off the excess acetate. Glue the rust card to the lid, matching up the apertures carefully. Fold the 4cm folding papers to fold sequence 26 (see page 51), glue them together to create the assembly shown above, then glue this to the rust triangle on the lid. Cut two leaves from the gold metal then glue these to the box.

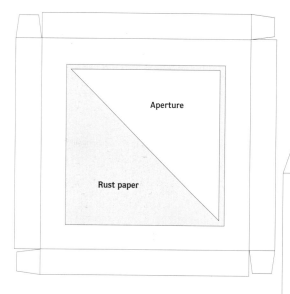

Aperture

Rust paper

Pattern for the Box project
Enlarge to 150%

LEAF AURORA

BIRDS CARD (See page 56)

Materials
Dark blue card (28 x 14cm)
Dark blue card (13.5cm square)
Pink and blue organza ribbon (2cm wide)
Silver wire
Wire mesh (8cm square)
5cm folding papers (eight)
Silver star sequins

Method
Use the matching rubber stamp and dark blue dye ink
to stamp a random design on the large blue card. Fold
the card to form a 14cm square, then cut a 10cm
aperture in the front of it and in the 13.5cm square
(the frame for the ribbon weaving). Weave the ribbons
(see page 9), then glue the frame to the inside front of
the card. Apply spots of glue in the middle of two
opposite sides of the mesh rubber (under where the
folded papers go), then place the wire mesh diagonally
on to the card. Bend the silver wire to make a freehand
zigzag zag with an eyelet at each end (see page
10),then glue it on to the wire mesh. Cut the 5cm
folding papers diagonally – the tip of the leaf shape
must be at the point of one of the triangles – then fold
eight similar triangles to fold sequence 29. Turn the
'bird' folds over, then glue two sets of four folds
together on the corners of the wire mesh. Finally, glue
on the silver sequins.

METAL AND MESH CARD (See page 56)

Materials
Dark blue card (27 x 13.5cm)
Dark blue card (11cm square)
Wire mesh (10cm square)
Silver coloured metal sheet (7cm square)
4cm folding papers (eight)
Folding paper (12cm square)
Blue, flat-back, jewellery stone (5mm diameter)

Method
Fold the large blue card to form a 13.5cm square, then
glue on the 12cm square of folding paper, the dark blue
square and the wire mesh. Use fancy-edged scissors to
cut the edges of the metal sheet, then, using the
matching stamp image, emboss the leaves (see page
10) on the back of the metal. Glue this to the wire

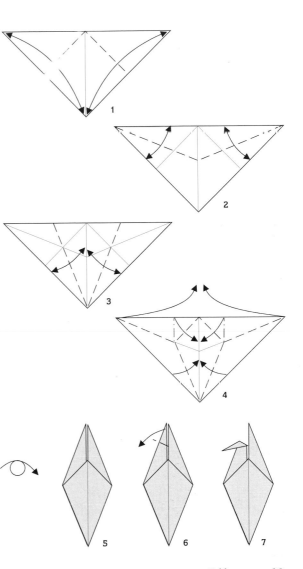

Fold sequence 29

mesh. Cut the folding papers diagonally, then fold eight
similar triangles to fold sequence 30 (see page 58).
Glue four of these in the middle of the card and the
other four in the corners. Finally glue the small
jewellery stone in the centre of the design.

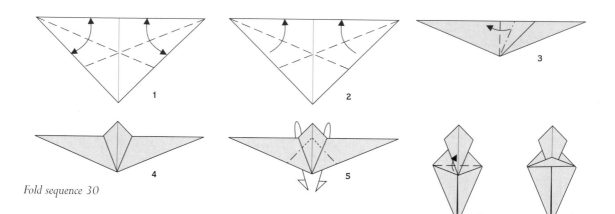

Fold sequence 30

MIRRORS CARD (See page 56)

Materials
Dark blue card (30 x 15cm)
Dark blue card (14cm square)
Wire mesh (9.5cm square)
Mirrors (two 2.5cm diameter)
Pink and blue organza ribbon (2cm wide)
4cm folding papers (sixteen)

Method
Fold the large blue card to form a 15cm square, then cut an 8cm aperture in it and in the dark blue square (the frame). Weave the ribbon diagonally across the frame (see page 9), then glue the frame to the inside front of the card. Cut the 4cm folding papers diagonally, then fold sixteen similar triangles to fold sequence 31. Use eight folds to build up a clockwise rosette, and the other eight to build up a counter-clockwise rosette. Glue the folds on to the mirrors, then use rubber solution adhesive to glue these to the wire mesh. Use double-sided sticky tape, (placed under the folds) to secure the wire mesh to the card.

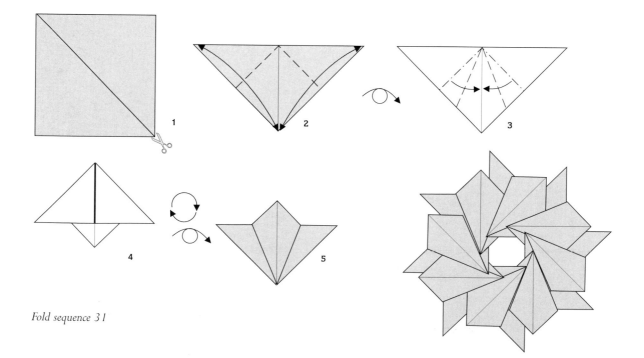

Fold sequence 31

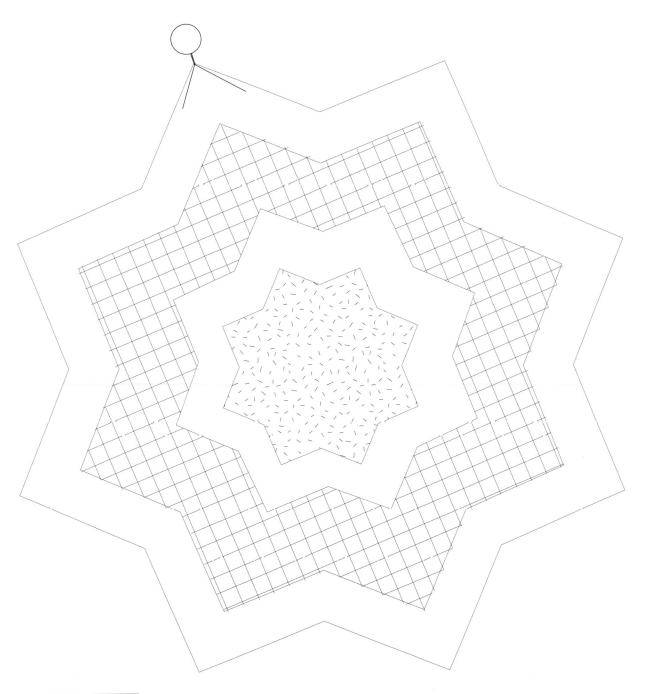

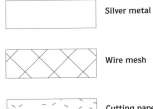

Silver metal

Wire mesh

Cutting paper

Pattern for the Star Suncatcher (see page 60)
Enlarge to 125%

PLASTIC BAUBLE (See page 57)

Materials
Clear plastic bauble with a separator (10cm diameter)
4cm folding papers (eight)

Method
Cut the 4cm folding papers diagonally so that the tip of the leaf shape is at the point of one of the triangles. Fold all sixteen triangles to step 5 of fold sequence 29 (see page 55) – eight of the finished folds will have one pattern, the other eight will have a similar, but slightly different pattern. Select eight similar folds, fold down the left-hand point of each (steps 6 and 7), then glue them together to make a rosette. On the other eight folds, turn down the right-hand point, then make a mirror-image rosette. Glue a rosette on each side of the separator, place this in the bauble and snap it shut.

STAR SUNCATCHER (See page 57)

Materials
Silver metal sheet (two, A4 sheets)
Wire mesh (A4 sheet)
Cutting paper
Silver wire
Blue, flat-back jewellery stone (two, 5mm diameter)

Method
Photocopy the pattern on page 59, then use this to cut out two large stars from the metal sheets; use a craft knife to cut round the inside edges first, then scissors to cut the outer edge. Cut the two centre star shapes from the waste metal. Emboss the stars (see page 10). Cut the wire mesh to a star shape, 1cm smaller all round than the large silver star. Place one of the large silver stars face down, then stick double-sided sticky tape around the inner edge. Remove the protective paper and lay the wire mesh star on this. Use the silver wire to make a hanger (see page 10), then glue this to one of the points of the silver star. Place more double-sided sticky tape around the outside edge of the star, then stick the other large silver star face up on top.

Cut a large patterned star shape, a small patterned star shape and two plain star shapes from the cutting paper. Use one of the plain star shapes as a guide to cut two small stars from the waste metal sheet. Emboss and cut these as described on page 29.

Glue the large patterned star shape to the centre metal star, then build up a layered, faux fold rosette with a plain star shape, a small metal star, a plain star shape, a small metal star and the small patterned star shape. Glue a jewellery stone in the middle of the rosette. Cut another set of shapes and make a second rosette. Use rubber solution adhesive to secure the finished star rosettes, back to back in the middle of the suncatcher.

SHERBET LEAF FANTASY

PAPER-PRICKED LEAVES CARD
(See front cover)

Materials
Pale green card (28 x 14cm)
Pale green card (11cm square)
Dark green card (12cm square)
Dark green card (6cm square)
Matching piece of origami paper
Cutting paper
4cm folding papers (two)

Method
Cut two plain shapes and one patterned shape from the cutting paper. Cut three star shapes (the same size as those above) from the origami paper. Fold and cut all the shapes for a faux fold rosette (see page 7). Layer the rosette, ending up with the patterned shape on top, then glue the whole rosette on to the 6cm square of dark green card. Trim the dark green card to the star shape leaving a small green border all round. Use the matching rubber stamp and dye ink to stamp two

images on to tracing paper. Use these images to paper prick leaf shapes on to the 11cm square of pale green card (see page 11). Fold the large pale green card to form a 14cm square, glue the 12cm square of dark

green card on to the folded card followed by the paper-pricked square and the rosette. Fold two half-papers to fold sequence 32, then glue the fold to the card as shown on the photograph.

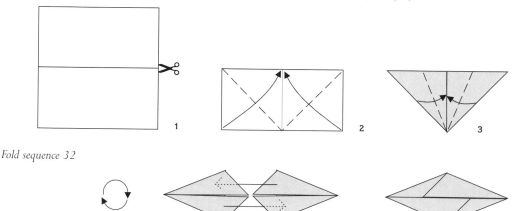

Fold sequence 32

STAR CARD (See page 61)

Materials
Dark red card (29 x 14.5cm)
Pink paper (12.5cm square)
4cm folding papers (eight)
Cutting paper
Gold sequins (eight, 3mm diameter)

Method
Use the matching rubber stamp and dark red dye ink to create a random pattern on the dark red card. Fold the card to form a 14.5cm square. Photocopy the pattern (see page 63) on to tracing paper, then, referring to page 11, paper prick the design on the pink paper – perforate all the straight lines from the front of the

paper, and the grey areas and the small circles from the back. Use fancy corner scissors to trim the corners of the pink paper, then glue it to the folded card. Cut the folding papers diagonally, then fold all sixteen triangles to fold sequence 33. Cut a plain multicoloured star shape from the cutting sheet, and glue it in the middle of the card. Glue eight similar folds together, then glue this rosette on the card so that its points align with those on the cutting paper star. Glue the other folds to the points of the paper-pricked star shape (the dotted lines on the pattern show their positions). Finally, glue the sequins between the points of the star shape.

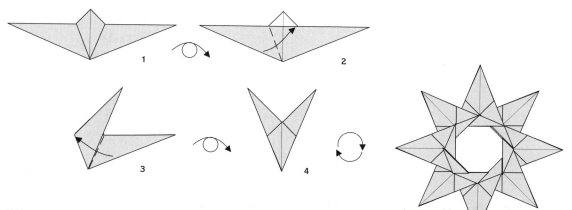

Fold sequence 33. Start from step 4 of fold sequence 30

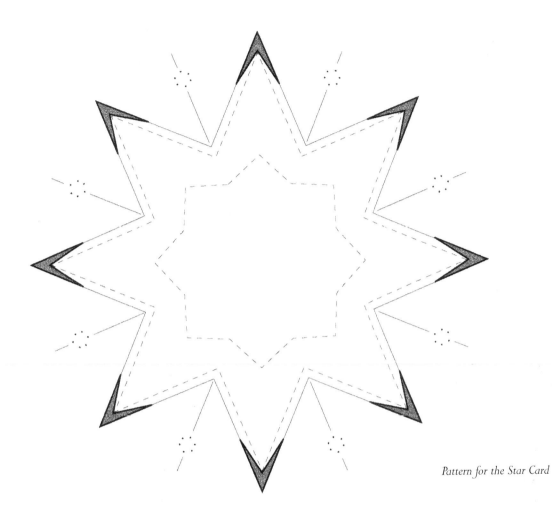

Pattern for the Star Card

WALL DECORATION (see page 61)

Materials
2mm thick card (two, 30cm squares)
Dark red paper (two, 32cm squares)
Pink (28cm square)
4cm folding papers (eight)
Cutting paper
Gold sequins (thirty-two, 3mm diameter)

Method
Cut a 24cm square aperture in one of the pieces of 2mm thick board, then glue it in the middle of the back of one of the dark red squares. Leaving a 1cm edge for turning in, cut out the centre of the paper. Mitre the inside and outside corners of the paper, then fold and glue the flaps on the back of the card to complete the frame. Glue the other piece of 2mm thick board to the back of the second piece of dark red paper, mitre the corners, then fold and glue the flaps to complete the back board. Use a matching rubber stamp and dark red dye ink to create a random design on the frame. Photocopy the pattern (see page 64) on to tracing paper then, referring to page 11), paper prick the design on to the pink paper – perforate all the lines from the front of the paper, then fill in the points and perforate the small circles from the back. Glue the paper pricking to the back board, then glue the frame over it.

The central design of folded papers is the same as that for the previous project, so refer to the relevant instructions on page 62.

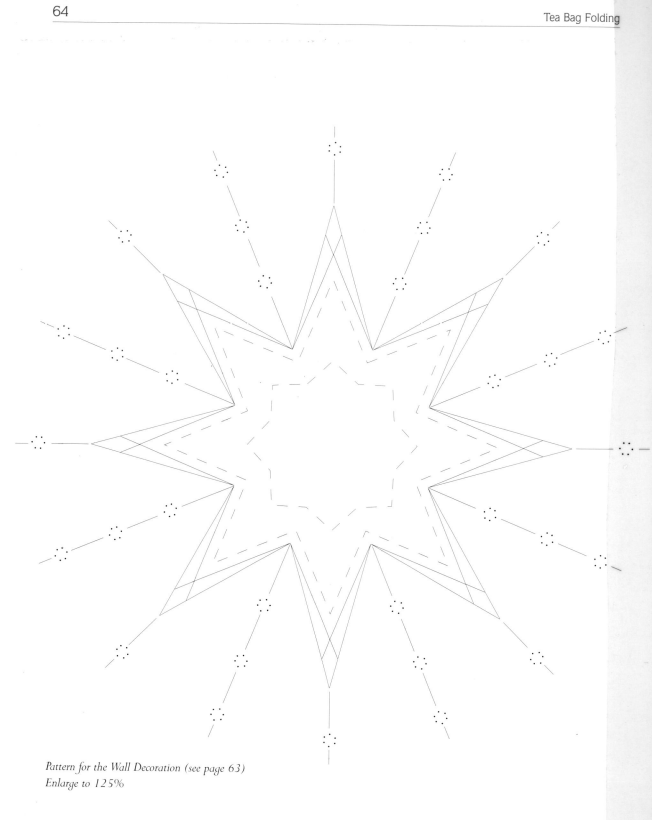

Pattern for the Wall Decoration (see page 63)
Enlarge to 125%